# Successful Communication at Work
## in a week

**JOHN MACDONALD**
**STEVE TANNER**

Hodder & Stoughton

A MEMBER OF THE HODDER HEADLINE GROUP

# Acknowledgments

The authors and publishers would like to thank the following for permission to quote from their work: Dr Faith Ralston and her publisher Amacom for material from her book *Hidden Dynamics* (see pages 26 – 27). Stuart Sillars and his publisher John Murray for material and the systems diagrams from his book *Success in Communication* (see pages 15 – 18).

Order queries: please contact Bookpoint Ltd, 39 Milton Park, Abingdon, Oxon OX14 4TD. Telephone: (44) 01235 400414, Fax: (44) 01235 400454. Lines are open from 9.00 - 6.00, Monday to Saturday, with a 24 hour message answering service. Email address: orders@bookpoint.co.uk

*British Library Cataloguing in Publication Data*
A catalogue record for this title is available from The British Library

ISBN 0 340 725052

First published 1997
Reissued 1998
Impression number   10  9  8  7  6  5  4  3  2  1
Year                2003  2002  2001  2000  1999  1998

Copyright © 1997 John Macdonald and Steve Tanner

All rights reserved. No part of this publication may be reproduced or transmitted in any form or by any means, electronic or mechanical, including photocopy, recording, or any information storage and retrieval system, without permission in writing from the publisher or under licence from the Copyright Licensing Agency Limited. Further details of such licences (for reprographic reproduction) may be obtained from the Copyright Licensing Agency Limited, of 90 Tottenham Court Road, London W1P 9HE.

Cover photo from Zefa Photo Library

Typeset by Multiplex Techniques Ltd, St Mary Cray, Kent.
Printed in Great Britain for Hodder & Stoughton Educational, a division of Hodder Headline Plc, 338 Euston Road, London NW1 3BH by Cox and Wyman, Reading, Berkshire.

The Institute of Management (IM) exists to promote the development, exercise and recognition of professional management. The Institute embraces all levels of management from student to chief executive and supports its own Foundation which provides a unique portfolio of services for all managers, enabling them to develop skills and achieve management excellence.

For information on the various levels and benefits of membership, please contact:

Department HS
Institute of Management
Cottingham Road
Corby
Northants NN17 1TT
Tel: 01536 204222
Fax: 01536 201651

This series is commissioned by the Institute of Management Foundation.

The authors can be contacted at:

129 Holly Lane East, Banstead, Surrey SM7 2BE.
Tel: 01737 373 552 Fax: 01737 373 557

# CONTENTS

| | | |
|---|---|---|
| **Introduction** | | 5 |
| **Sunday** | The key to business success | 7 |
| **Monday** | Barriers to communication | 21 |
| **Tuesday** | Technology and media | 33 |
| **Wednesday** | Customer focus | 47 |
| **Thursday** | Employee focus | 62 |
| **Friday** | External communication | 78 |
| **Saturday** | Keep talking and listening | 90 |

# INTRODUCTION

Communication with customers, employees, suppliers, shareholders and the community at large is what business is all about. It lies at the heart of current performance-improvement initiatives such as total quality management, business process re-engineering and benchmarking. Communication is a process which applies equally to manufacturing, service and public-sector organisations. Successful communication at work is now a global issue.

This has already been called 'The Age of Communication'. Technology has created a rapidly increasing ability for an ever larger number of people to communicate relatively freely with one another. Yet that very freedom to communicate, allied with the constant increase in the pace and amount of communication, has exposed a series of barriers to successful communication. What once appeared to be a simple process has now become a complex and confusing issue for those involved in work.

# INTRODUCTION

The aim of this book is to dispel the confusion and to provide a logical guide to achieving successful communication at work.

| | |
|---|---|
| **Sunday** | Understanding communication |
| **Monday** | Recognising the barriers |
| **Tuesday** | Media and message |
| **Wednesday** | Listening to customers |
| **Thursday** | Permission to communicate |
| **Friday** | Involving others |
| **Saturday** | It's good to talk and listen |

# SUNDAY

## The key to business success

Everyone at work is involved in communication in some form or another. We talk and write to our customers, and sometimes actually listen to them. We also communicate in many ways with our colleagues, and with a multitude of people in other organisations on whom we depend for our ultimate success. If any of these communication channels break down or our messages are misunderstood, we risk disruption or even a failure to meet our objectives. And while we are wrestling with our communication problems, a competitor, with better communication, can then slip in and sign the sales contract. Clear, concise and timely communication is thus the key to business success.

Unfortunately, before we start work, few of us are taught to communicate in a manner best suited to business. This is because we all learn to communicate in a social rather than a business environment.

# SUNDAY

Our early experience of communication is in a relaxed atmosphere with a wide latitude in expression and vocabulary. Usually, the parties to communication here know each other well and will therefore have an innate understanding of each other's perceptions and attitudes. In this environment, much can be left unsaid or paraphrased because it will be taken 'as read'. Equally, there is no pressure to hurry or to weigh every word carefully. Miscommunication here is unlikely to incur the same penalties as it can in business. Most social communication is informal and spoken, though occasionally, social communication will also demand some formality, particularly at times of condolence or celebration. In the social environment, these latter occasions are the nearest that most will come to the precision and accuracy demanded in business communication.

# SUNDAY

## Business is different

In the business environment, communication plays a vital role in ensuring that things get done. To avoid costly misunderstandings and time delays, communication here has to be clear, concise and direct. You also need to ensure that whoever you communicate to is listening and wants to hear what you have to say. Business communication is thus formal in nature, and must be carefully planned and organised to be successful.

The contrast between social and business communication is well expressed by Stuart Sillars. In social communication, the telephone is an instrument for having a chat, while in business communication, it is a way to convey information quickly and perhaps cheaply. Social letters are full of personal news and are informal in language and style, whereas business letters contain only essential factual information, are much shorter and use a more formal – though not completely impersonal – style. Social talk is unhurried, uses slang and expressions understood only by small groups, and often does not follow any grammatical sentence structure. Business talk, on the other hand, should be carefully planned, should be carried out quickly as time is valuable, uses no slang – although it may use specialised language – and should be grammatical in its construction. In short, business communication is planned in its layout and expression and composed according to clear objectives, whereas social communication follows no rigid structure and may be quite spontaneous. We shall return to these contrasts throughout the week.

# SUNDAY

## Understanding communication

We cannot plan and organise our business communication unless we fully understand the issues involved. The communications model shown will help to illustrate the various elements involved in all communication:

- Parties to the communication: sender and receiver
- Direct channels
- Indirect channels
- Interference

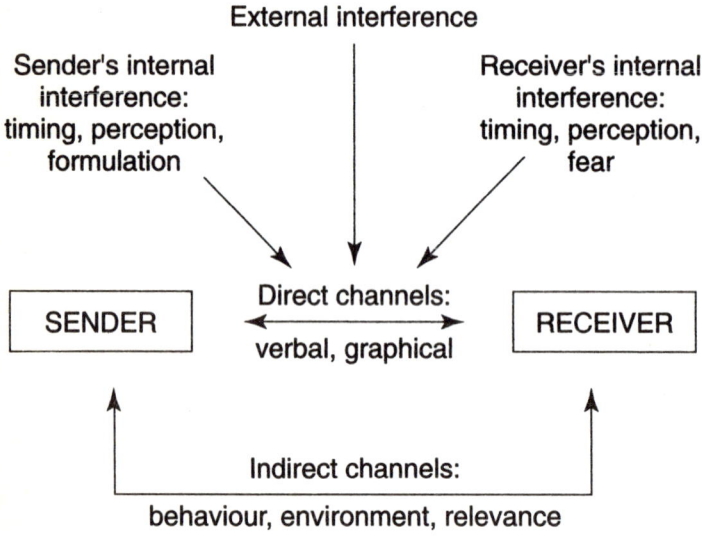

Figure 1: *Communications model*

We will look at each of these elements in turn.

## SUNDAY

*Parties to the communication*

Communication requires a minimum of two parties to the transaction. Usually, one party is cast in the role of the *sender* or initiator of the message, and the other in the role of the *receiver* of the message. However, in successful communication, both parties play both roles. Our model shows an arrow head at *both* ends of the *communication channel* through which messages are conveyed. In other words, the sender requires *feedback* from the receiver to confirm that the transaction was completed. This feedback can be seen as a new message with the roles reversed. Confusion or miscommunication can result from *interference* in each direction.

*Direct channels*

In communications theory, channels have little or nothing to do with the technology or media used. Rather, they relate to the form of the message. For example, the most commonly used channel in business communication is verbal i.e. by way of words. Verbal communication can be transmitted orally, by writing or visually – as for example on a computer terminal.

A further essential element of business communication is graphic – i.e. involves images. Architects' and engineers' drawings are good examples of this form of communication. The visual image is the most powerful form of direct communication, and one which modern technology is able to enhance in the business enviornment. A picture, as they say, is worth a thousand words!

The *direct channels* are those modes of communication that the sender and hopefully the receiver *select* for their exchange of information.

# SUNDAY

*Indirect channels*

Indirect channels of communication are the most ignored element in the planning of business communication. That may be the reason that the information conveyed through indirect channels is the major source of inadequate, misleading or disruptive messages in the workplace. However, these channels can also provide a powerful reinforcement of the intended message.

The communications model on page 10 notes behaviour, environment and relevance as examples of indirect channels. Each of these factors includes a host of subsidiary messages or items of information that accompany the main message. For example, a speech delivered in a boring, monotone voice and with a sloppy or indifferent body language would convey indirect messages that run counter to the 'exciting' language of the new product launch that forms the content of that speech. In the same way, a manager who distributes a memo on the importance of quality that has been badly photocopied and has dark smudges and unaligned text will again disrupt that message.

Our body language, our choice of words or idioms relevant to the message, and our handling of the media are all indirect messages that can support or detract from the real message. These indirect messages are present at all times, and in a sense provide the framework for the interpretation of the information conveyed. They also provide an important clue about the integrity of the sender, and thus about the degree of relevance of the specific communication. The indirect channels are related to the differences we discussed earlier between social and business communication.

# SUNDAY

*Interference*
*Interference*, or 'noise in the channel', prevents a message from being transmitted or received in the manner or the significance intended.

The most obvious form is *external interference*. Savage heckling or platform colleagues muttering during a speech are examples of external interference. So also would be a major news break (e.g. an earthquake or declaration of war) on the very day that you are announcing a new product. The financial collapse of a major customer referenced in the announcement would also constitute an external interference to the message being conveyed. Although planned communication should take any possible external interferences into account, it is never easy to control.

*Internal interference* is a different matter, and its elimination is a key element in successful communication. This form of interference is a major contributor to creating the barriers to

## SUNDAY

communication that we will discuss on Monday. In principle, internal interference relates to perceptions held by both the sender and the receiver. The perception that the sender has of the relevance of the message to the intended recipient, who may be inside or external to the company, will play a large part in the formulation of the message. The receiver's perception in turn is likely to be influenced by past experience. In the case of an employee, the perception of the message may be tinged with fear. In the case of the weary customer, the purport of the message may be endangered by a cynical perception of the company.

The communications model shown above can help us both to prevent the negative aspects of business communication, and to plan positively for direct and successful communication. In principle, we are striving for an identity of purpose and perception between the sender and the recipient. An understanding of this model and this identity should be the basis for all communication systems used in the workplace.

## Communication systems

The rapid increase in the pace and amount of communication has led both to increased complexity and, often, to a breakdown in communications. As a result, modern organisations have developed systems or networks for the management of communication.

*Group networks*
In small organisations, the communication systems are simple and direct, though they may still suffer from 'noise in the channel'. In large organisations, it is often necessary to define clearly responsibility and accountability, which in

# SUNDAY

turn will determine who speaks to whom. Chaos could easily result from a lack of definition here, since messages with unclear destinations can be lost or ignored. Messages requiring action from the recipients need to be delivered to the right people in a timely fashion. For this reason, groups of defined communication networks are formed within the organisation. These groups may manage specific elements of the business or be established to simplify and speed up communication.

*The open network*
In this system every member of the group may communicate with every other member, so that all channels of communication are open. Generally, this works best for a fairly small group or team where the members know each other, can work well together and are often multi-skilled and multi-tasked.

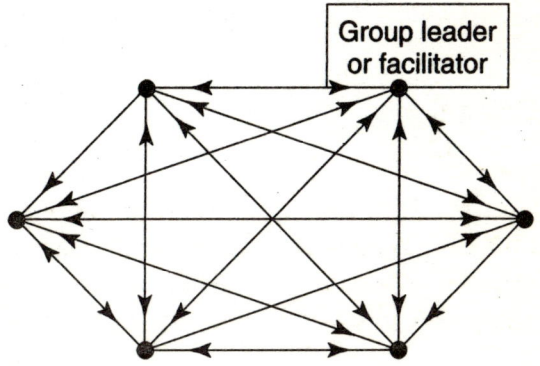

● Group member

Figure 2: *The open network*

## SUNDAY

*The Y system*
This system is also suitable for a small group, but differs from the open system in that it directs communication along very clear channels. Here, one person co-ordinates information from various levels.

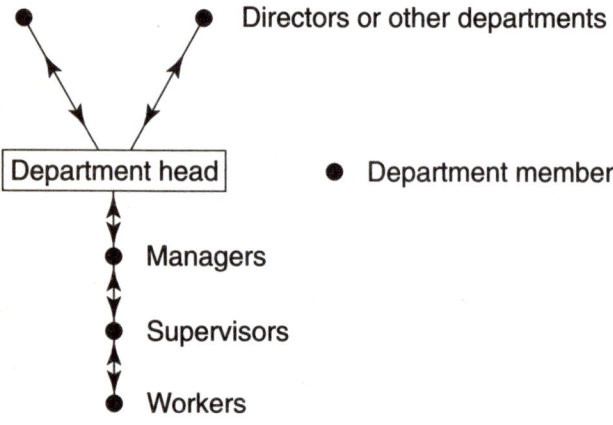

Figure 3: *The Y system*

*The fan system*
Fan systems are most commonly used in large organisations, to ensure that communication takes place only through very clearly defined channels, namely through supervisors and managers. The advantage of this system is that a clear pattern of communication is created, which saves time. The disadvantage is that the group becomes very rigid, with divisions encouraged between peer groups and levels of employees. This is a controlling rather than an empowering system.

# SUNDAY

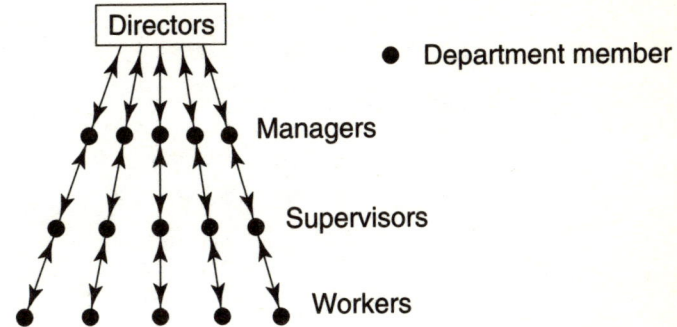

Figure 4: *The fan system*

*The daisy system*
This is a typical management system used for a number of individuals reporting to a central group. It is direct and simple, but has the disadvantage of removing levels of employees from the communication.

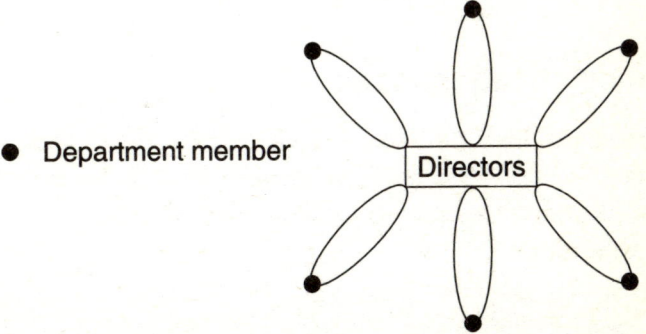

Figure 5: *The daisy system*

*The combination network*

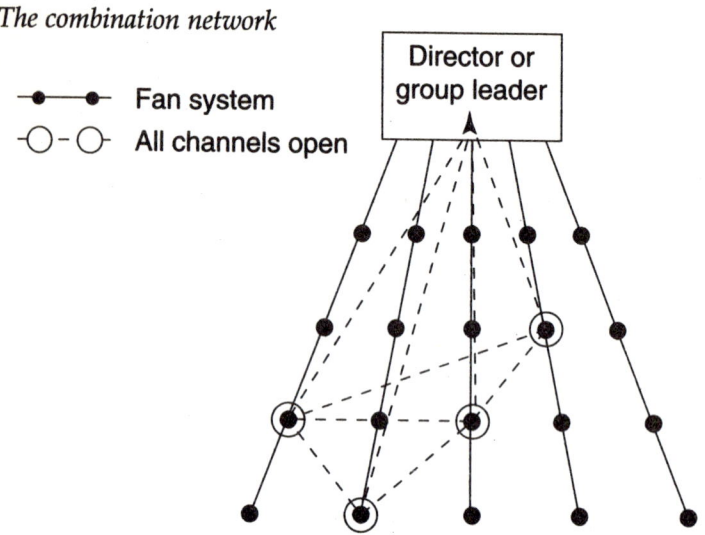

Figure 6: *The combination network*

Increasingly, the structured systems which provide a direct exchange of information are combined with the 'permission' to network in a combined system. This provides maximum flexibility and efficiency.

## Communication issues

These basic descriptions of systems and the broad theory of communication have made little mention of the major communication issues facing the management of organisations:

- Competitive pressure on a global scale
- The changing perceptions of customers
- The rising expectations of employees

# SUNDAY

- Language and cultural issues
- The sheer amount of information
- The impact of technology

Each day we will consider these issues from a different perspective.

## The purpose of communication

We mentioned earlier that businesses require clear, concise and direct communication to *get things done*. Unfortunately, this is far from common practice in modern organisations. A consultant was advising a large corporation involved in the packaging industry. He had been impressed with the participatory management style evident in the corporate offices. On a visit to an operational location, he asked the plant manager what he thought of the open and frank communication style in the corporation. The reply was illuminating: 'In this company we communicate openly and frankly about everything – except about making boxes.' And of course 'making boxes' was their business. In a sense, this book is about communicating to help us to make boxes – indeed to make the very best boxes that will delight our potential customers.

To achieve that, we must also achieve two way communication with our customers; both to understand their needs and to inform them that we have what they want. Later in the week we will consider the implications of successful communication with the wider community in which business is involved.

# SUNDAY

## Summary

Today, we have looked at the principles of communication and talked about some of the communication systems commonly used in organisations. For the rest of the week, we will concentrate on eliminating the barriers to successful communication and developing positive approaches to our communication needs. We can summarise Sunday as follows:

- We are all involved in communication
- Clear, concise and direct communication is the key
- We learn to communicate in a social environment
- Business communication is different from social communication
- There are direct and indirect channels of communication
- We must eliminate interferences to communication
- We must strive to achieve an identity of purpose and perception between the sender and the recipient
- We use many defined systems of communication
- We should communicate in order to get things done

On Monday, we will look at eliminating the barriers to communication.

# MONDAY

# Barriers to communication

Current management practices inhibit clear, concise and direct communication of the information needed to get things done successfully. Some of them create barriers to communication between each level of management as well as between departmental peers at each level. Other barriers are created by the individual perceptions of the parties to communication, and by the fostered cultures of organisations. The major barriers to communication can be summarised as:

- Specialisation and departmental fortresses
- The division between the thinkers and the doers
- Tradition, culture and status
- Hidden dynamics – emotions at work
- National myopias and perceptions
- The lack of a common language

## Specialisation

Modern industry is said to have begun when Frederick Taylor and others convinced businessmen that if they divided major processes or work activities into a host of small specialised activities, they could achieve massive increases in productivity. These pioneers of modern industry were proved right, and the era of mass production began. But conditions changed, and the process of *specialisation* created other problems which were not recognised at the time.

# MONDAY

One result of pursuing the 'truth' of specialisation has been the steady division of business operations both horizontally and vertically: a horizontal division between departmental functions, and a vertical division between 'the thinkers' and 'the doers'. Over time, each such division has created barriers both to communication and to an understanding of how the business is operating. The phenomenon of 'them and us' is much broader than the division between managers and workers.

## Departmental fortresses

Organisations manage people and work through functional departments. The managers and people within these departments communicate well with each other but are dedicated to their own objectives only. Often, their objectives are divisive, so that departments compete, rather than collaborate, with each other. This traditional system has created 'departmental fortresses' causing barriers to communication across the organisation. Ultimately in this environment, an organisation sees its customers and

# MONDAY

suppliers as combatants to be overcome. Process-oriented communication, which is based on measurement and getting things done, is what must replace fortress communication. We shall look at this area in depth on Thursday.

## The division between the thinkers and the doers

The major elements of the style of management based on specialisation were command, control and compliance. Jobs were designed so that each worker had one highly repetitive task, and jobs that required many skills were replaced by narrowly defined jobs in which supervisors made all the decisions. The worker didn't have to think: he or she just had to be controlled. This division between the 'thinkers' and the 'doers' has persisted to this day. Yet in modern industry, the repetitive non-thinking jobs are being eliminated or carried out by machines and workers are thus being asked to return to a multi-skilled thinking process in work; in today's jargon, they are being 'empowered'. Unfortunately, however, the traditional controlling instincts remain as another barrier to successful communication.

*Corporate chateaux*
As the channels of communication and action became more complex and time-consuming, the thinkers needed people to advise them and to help control the disparate elements of the business. These advisors are organised into staff groups who exercise power and control on behalf of executives. Their 'customer' is senior management rather than the actual customer of the business. As the eyes, ears and voice of management, they serve to reinforce the separation between management and worker. Even more important, this trend has divided management both from

communication with the customer and from the real issues of the marketplace.

In most businesses today, a substantial proportion of managers and employees have little or no contact with the customer or with the people who make products or deliver service. They live in 'corporate chateaux' (like the generals in the Great War) and spend their working hours with other managers or 'members of staff'. They are far removed from changing customer perceptions, the 'insignificant' problems of the workers and 'difficult' customers. Too often, their energy is expended on jockeying for political position and extending their own privileges rather than on improving the business.

## Tradition, culture and status

Only too often, and despite their best attempts at a successful communication strategy, most executives fail to see the hidden barriers to communication based on individual perceptions of tradition, culture and status.

Individuals will formulate or interpret a message according to their own perception of 'what goes on around here' or 'what they really meant'. New executives may not recognise that a long tradition of authoritarian communications from on-high has established a cynical mistrust of all management messages. Customers of a public utility may not trust the statements of a perceived 'fat cat'. These perceptions can actually create gaps in communication because the intended recipients 'turn off' and do not listen to the message. In our prevailing organisational culture, executives, managers and employees all exhibit behaviour patterns which create these gaps:

# MONDAY

*Executives*
- will often communicate decisions with little or no knowledge of the implication of their decisions for the company or the people who have to implement the decisions
- fail to communicate effectively – they are bad at explaining decisions
- send *different* messages to shareholders and staff respectively
- work as individuals, not as teams. They call for teamwork throughout the organisation, but they exclude themselves from this
- rarely 'walk as they talk'. In other words, they exhort the workforce to adhere to values which they themselves blatantly ignore
- fail to establish measurable criteria for anything other than short-term financial or people management. Therefore, they do not know what is going on
- fail to lead. They are all too often remote from their organisations

*Managers*
- feel stressed or overstretched in implementing executive decisions
- lack enthusiasm for change – they have been let down before
- fail to collaborate or to practice teamwork with their peers
- create a 'purposeful fog' which inhibits communication
- ape the executives in actions, a lack of measurement and a failure to lead

*Employees*
- are left in the dark, victims of the mushroom management joke
- feel at the bottom of the pit with no one left to hit
- feel scepticism and mistrust
- feel unheard and unappreciated
- are unable, as a result, to release their potential, and tend to construct a 'defence mechanism'

These behaviour patterns are based on perceptions or beliefs which are themselves assumptions about what is true. The trouble with organisational behaviour is that such perceptions quickly become facts, because people tend to communicate and act within the framework of their perceptions.

## Hidden dynamics – emotions at work

The traditional 'rational' world of business believes that our emotions are better kept private. Faith Ralston argues that this is a dangerous misconception, and that, like it or not, human feelings affect every job and organisation. Too often at work, we try to stifle our feelings, and yet, even in a business environment, our emotional needs can be harnessed for positive communication and positive results.

To understand and to deal with the dynamic nature of emotions in the workplace, the following eight principles are important to keep in mind:

1 Emotional needs always express themselves one way or another.
2 Anger is an expression of need.

# MONDAY

3  Our feelings and needs are not wrong or bad.
4  Emotions are the gateway to vitality and feeling alive.
5  We can address our emotions and still save face.
6  Immediate reactions to problems often disguise deeper feelings.
7  We must clarify individual needs before problem-solving with others.
8  We need to communicate both positive and negative feelings.

## National myopias and perceptions

National cultures or the particular use of language can create major blind spots or false perceptions which hinder clear, concise and direct communication by large corporations. In most cases, the perpetrators of these communication blunders remain in blissful ignorance of the damage they are causing. They are imprisoned in a

# MONDAY

'national myopia'. The vast need for an increase in global communication in business highlights this as an area of growing concern in successful communication.

We have all laughed from time to time at bizarre stories of international miscommunication. These mishaps are usually obvious, but there are a host of others that go unrecognised by the senders and so continue to sow discord or misconception. Some examples will suffice to make the point.

- The English play cricket, as do a large number of English-speaking countries (but not the USA). However, expressions such as 'a sticky wicket' and 'keeping a straight bat' have little place in business communication
- The Americans play baseball (which most of the rest of the world, however, does not – despite the fact that the Americans refer to it as the 'world series') and their own form of football. As a result, constant references to the importance of the 'quarterback' or to being 'out in left field' fall on deaf ears

# MONDAY

- In Western countries, the term 'bureaucrat' is perjorative. In India and other Eastern countries, however, it simply means a civil servant or a member of the government
- Most national cultures have evolved *norms* or unwritten prescriptive rules for business communication. This is dangerous trap for the unwary in 'collaborative' ventures

## The lack of a common language

An area of language difficulty in business communication that is not so readily recognised are the different 'languages' used by executives, management and workers. Executives are reputed to be concerned about only three issues: (i) making money, (ii) not losing money, and (iii) money! Although this is perhaps not totally fair, it does serve to illustrate a serious issue in internal business communication. Workers on their part do *not* talk in the language of money, but instead in the language of things and getting things done. They may be interested in the worth of their pay packet, but they are not much concerned with revenue and profit ratios. Yet too often executives will talk to workers in the language of business finance and assume that the latter should know what is happening. Middle managers are caught in between as they attempt to talk both languages and often just end up confusing everybody.

To achieve purposeful communication within organisations, we need to use a common language to overcome the barriers of status or function. The most successful organisations use the language of processes and measurement to communicate effectively about 'making boxes' or getting things done. We will look at this area in more depth on Thursday.

## Management communication

Work is carried out in a series of processes which flow across an organisation to provide an eventual product or service to a customer. Each of the individual processes in the flow has its own customer and supplier. For most people working in an organisation, their direct customer is another individual or process in the organisation, and this customer may well be in another department or location. The essential issue is that the ultimate customer is dependent on the weakest link in that chain of processes for his or her satisfaction or hopefully delight. For this reason, the essential objective of management direction and communication should be to ensure the success of these processes. However, as the diagram below illustrates, management communication is concentrated on departments rather than on processes. In this situation, management has established its own barrier to success.

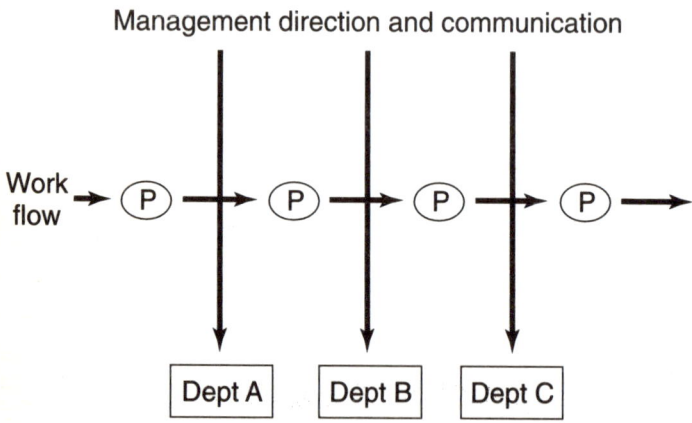

Figure 7: *Management direction and communication*

# MONDAY

This barrier also affects the essential area of establishing requirements. As we noted earlier, each process in a chain has its own customers and suppliers. The essential communication in that chain should be about the customer's requirements and then the requirements on the supplier to meet the first objective. A moment's thought will indicate that meeting requirements entails resources. Only management has the power to disperse resources, and so management must play a key part in establishing the requirements for a process. As the diagram below illustrates, the failure to establish and communicate clear requirements creates its own barrier to success. Probably 85 per cent of the errors in business are caused by a lack of clear requirements.

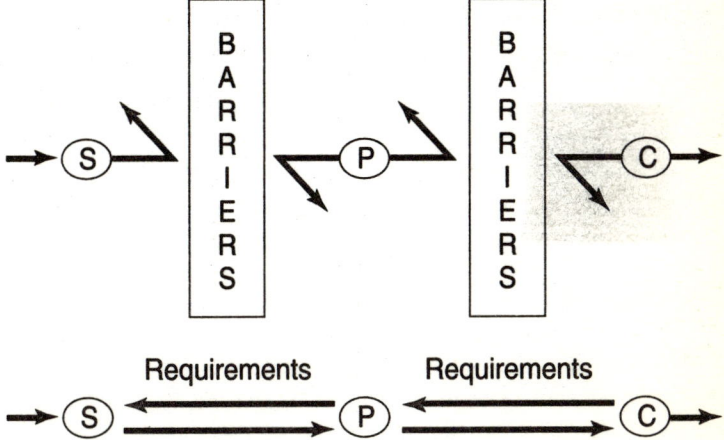

Figure 8: *More barriers*

# ■■■■■ M O N D A Y ■■■■■

## Education and training

The difficulties caused by the transition from social to business communication which we noted on Sunday, are exacerbated by weaknesses in education, training and the induction of employees. The whole area of standards in education is now a matter of debate in most countries and lies outside the scope of this book. However, the continuation of the educational process within the business environment is a crucial issue for successful communication.

The current level of resource devoted to the development and training of employees in most companies is lamentable. It is probably the greatest barrier to successful communication that exists in business. Employers really do have to learn that the cost of ignorance far exceeds the price of education and training. In that context there is a need for a greater emphasis on induction or transition to help all to adjust to the needs of business. What came naturally with apprenticeship or 'articled pupils' and the foundation year at college, has never been replaced.

## Summary

Today we have looked at a series of barriers that exist, or that management create, that inhibit clear and concise communication. Over the week, we will examine positive actions designed to remove these barriers. Tomorrow, on Tuesday, we shall focus on the methods and media used to communicate in business.

# T U E S D A Y

# Technology and media

A radically changing world is altering the way we work, the way we communicate and what we communicate about. We have entered the 'Information Age'. A few facts will help us to understand first the changes in technology and then the impact that it has had on the way in which we work.

## Changes in technology

- In 1991, for the first time ever, companies spent more money on computing and communications equipment than the combined amount spent on industrial, mining, and construction equipment
- ENIAC, the world's first computer, was built in 1944. It took up more space than two double-decker buses and consumed 140,000 watts of electricity. ENIAC could execute up to 5,000 basic arithmetic operations per second
- A modern 486 microprocessor, is built on a silicon chip about the size of a fingernail. It weighs less than a tea bag, and uses less than 2 watts of electricity. A 486 can execute up to 54,000,000 instructions per second
- The development of the integrated circuit has permitted an ever-increasing amount of information to be stored or processed on a single microchip. This is what has driven the information revolution
- Between 1960 and 1970, the number of components on a microchip doubled each year from 1 in 1960 to 1,000 in 1970. The pace has since increased reaching 100,000,000 in 1990 and 1,000,000,000 in 1992

# TUESDAY

- Computer power is now 8,000 times less expensive than it was 30 years ago. If we had similar progress in motor cars, you could now buy a Lexus for £2, it would travel at the speed of sound and it would consume a thimble of petrol for every 600 miles
- Since 1990, more than 12,000,000 computers have been sold in the UK
- The number of mobile-telephone users in the UK has jumped from zero in 1982 to over 4,000,000 in 1995
- Close to 800,000 people now carry pagers, and an estimated 30,000,000 messages were left in electronic mailboxes in the UK in 1994 alone
- Between 1985 and 1995, offices and homes in the UK installed some 1,700,000 fax machines
- The first practical industrial robot was introduced during the 1960s. By 1982, there were approximately 32,000 robots in use in the USA; that has now risen to over 20,000,000.

# TUESDAY

Communication technology is radically changing the speed, direction and amount of information flow, even as it also alters work roles all across organisations. As a case in point, the number of secretaries has dropped by more than 20 per cent in the last ten years.

## Growth in information

- There has been more information produced in the last 30 years than was produced during the previous 5,000
- A single edition of *The Times* contains more information than the average person met in a lifetime in the 17th century
- The information supply available to us doubles every 5 years, and the pace is increasing
- Electronic mail (E-mail) and the Internet have broken down barriers to information growth by creating open ownership of information and free knowledge transfer
- Video and audio E-mail, and now video conferencing using PCs and the Internet, are further breaking down international barriers and eliminating the problem of distance between communicating parties.

## Changes in the way we work

- As recently as the 1960s, almost one half of all workers in the industrialised countries were involved in making things
- By the year 2000, no developed country will have more than one-sixth or even one-eighth of its workforce in traditional roles of making and moving goods
- Already, an estimated two-thirds of American employees work in the services sector

# TUESDAY

- By the year 2000, less than half the workforce in the developed countries will be holding conventional full-time jobs in organisations.
- Every year, more and more people will be self-employed, or will work on a temporary or part-time basis; sometimes from desire, sometimes because that is all that is available.

In this new age, *knowledge* is becoming the most important product. Communication will be less about instructions and more about exchanging information so as to increase the power of our knowledge. This calls for different organisations, as well as different kinds of worker.

Another book in this series, *Understanding Business Process Re-engineering*, included a list of technologies which would be critical to future communication in business, as follows:

| | |
|---|---|
| Document image processing | New database technologies |
| Client service architecture | Co-operative processing |
| Work-group applications | Executive information systems |
| Process-based systems | Expert systems |
| Electronic data interchange | Local area networks |
| Facsimiles | Card-reading devices |
| Bar coding | Graphical interfaces |

# TUESDAY

Others were also noted, but this is not the place to describe all the trends in future technology. However, it is clear that successful communication in tomorrow's business will be impacted by technology. The business environment will require a substantial investment in multi-skill education and training. An essential element in the whole change process is to ensure that managers and people have a growing comprehension of the contribution technology can make to helping them communicate successfully. Before leaving technology, we should say something about the information superhighway.

## The information superhighway

The information superhighway is a name coined by the US American vice-president Al Gore to bring together a host of communications and computing technologies. A vast amount of investment in high-capacity cables and networks is required to provide the essential infrastructure. When it does come, however, it will be a high-capacity, two-way digital communications link that will connect providers of information with consumers throughout the world.

In the meantime, the Internet is the closest parallel we have to a superhighway.

## The Internet

Most users of the Internet, both at the office and in the home, work from computers with 'Windows' screen displays. The information is displayed as a colourful mixture of text and graphics. Users 'surf the net' by moving the mouse cursor to items of interest and then clicking the button. Each click takes the user to a new location (which may be thousands of miles away) on the Internet. The mechanics of the Internet are very similar to those of the superhighway. The principal difference, however, is the capacity of the communications link.

In both the Internet and the superhighway, consumers send requests to providers, who then deliver the information or goods either back down the link or by more conventional methods. The superhighway will be able to carry entertainment as well as information. Films will be transmitted as well as electronic mail, faxes and person-to-person communications including voice and video phone. The superhighway will connect people to people, people to information and computers to computers.

Individuals will now be able to lay their hands on information more quickly, and businesses will be able to make their product literature and publicity material available to the rest of the world at a fraction of the cost of delivering it by conventional means.

## Media and message

In many instances in modern technology, it is difficult to escape the conclusion that the media has become more important than the message. All too often, senders are more concerned to demonstrate their prowess with the latest technology than they are to ensure that the recipient has received and understood the intended message. Having said that, an essential element of successful communication is the selection and use of the media best suited to both the message and the recipients.

## TUESDAY

The communication model on page 10 above can provide a helpful reference guide when planning large-scale communication such as conferences and advertising. Some typical examples of the misuse or bad selection of media that create interference will serve to illustrate the point:

- The use of overhead transparencies coupled with standard-sized screens at large conferences. No one but the speaker can see a thing, and the message is lost
- Over-crowded transparencies, which produce the same result, at any kind of event
- The back or forward projection of 35 mm slides controlled by separate operators using a scripted speech. In concentrating on not missing the keywords the speaker loses all spontaneity and rapport with the audience
- TV and other advertisements which appear to be competing for 'in group' prizes rather than selling the product to the target buyers. The message here is drowned in clever visual tricks and layouts

- E-mail messages or memos that are sent indiscriminately to 'complete' lists without reference to their relevance to each individual recipient. These create so much 'noise in the channel' that important messages are obscured
- Over-reliance on the ability of technology to handle error correction with ease, which is conducive to a lazy and bad formulation of messages, and to the expectation that someone else will spot errors and make the relevant corrections. In some organisations, the major impact of computers has been just to move communication errors around both more quickly and to a wider audience. 'Right first time' should be a principle of all communication.

## Technical jargon

The growing influence of technology has ushered in a quasi-scientific language for business communication. Each functional specialisation now has its own brand of management sciences or jargon, with which to confound its internal competitors. Much of this new language is incomprehensible, but few managers are prepared to admit openly that they don't understand the new terminology. Business has stolen the emperor's clothes!

## Communication methodology

Successful business communication depends on a clear methodology which we have been developing since starting on Sunday. This methodology is based on three principles:

# TUESDAY

> 1 Understanding the category, characteristics and environment of the intended recipient of our messages
> 2 Selecting the ideal media both to fit the message content and to meet the recipient's needs
> 3 Formulating the message and the form of presentation so as to maximise the advantages of the selected media

This methodology presupposes that the message is worthwhile and that the recipient is predisposed to receive the message. The above principles are not intended to be a form of bureaucratic procedure to be followed for every message we wish to communicate in day-to-day business operations. Rather, they should be seen as an element in a thinking process that should become automatic.

*Understanding the recipient*
A lack of comprehension of the first principle above probably accounts for the majority of mistakes in business communication. The higher we rise in the organisational hierarchy, the more likely we are to send messages that are doomed to be misunderstood. The senior manager may have a message that he or she wants to convey to all those involved in an issue. In the haste to communicate in a timely fashion, the disparate characteristics of the recipients and the environments in which they work are ignored. Or perhaps, more typically, the message is adulterated and compromised for a wider audience. The perception of each category of recipient is different, and as a result, the message is perceived in a number of different ways. The issue becomes clearer when we appreciate the differing

# TUESDAY

characteristics and working environments of all the following normal recipients of some form of business communication:

| | |
|---|---|
| owners | shareholders |
| boards of directors | senior managers |
| managers and supervisors | specialists and technologists |
| corporate staff | field staff |
| sales force | sales support staff |
| administrative workers | manufacturing workers |
| key material suppliers | in-house service suppliers |
| other suppliers | consultants |
| key account customers | prospects |
| other customers | trade associations |
| the trade press | other press and media |
| regulatory bodies | local government |
| central government | the community |

Additionally, in this politically correct world, we have to take account of gender, nationality, race and even sexual proclivities. If that was not enough, we also have to consider the overall communication environment before we select our media. Some of the possibilities involved are noted overleaf:

# TUESDAY

| | |
|---|---|
| one-to-one | selected groups |
| en masse | face-to-face |
| direct | indirect |
| verbal | visual image |
| one-off | repetitive |
| natural environment | designed environment |

In the language of communication, the bottom two here are often referred to as 'your place or mine.'

*Choice of media*

The modern business communicator has access to a wide choice of media for distributing a message. In theory, this should assist in matching the right kind of media both to the message and to the recipient. In practice, however, it is not as simple as that. Many of the media listed below need skilled interpreters and/or are not in the control of the principal communicator:

| | |
|---|---|
| the national press and TV | the local press and TV |
| in-house magazines | the trade press |
| in-house conferences/seminars | external conferences |
| team briefings | staff/union meetings |
| memorandum | E-mail/the internet |
| telephone | faxes |
| letters | 'business lunches' |
| committees | meetings |

# TUESDAY

All too often, the media is selected or appears opportune for use without due consideration of either the message or the targeted recipients. The above list of media is by no means exhaustive but, allied to the list of conceivable recipients, it does add to the seeming complexity of making 'mix and match' decisions.

*Formulating the message*

Formulate a clear purposeful message, and it may survive the wrong choice of media. Formulate a fuzzy message, and no clever devices of technology will suffice. The old adage of communication KISS ("Keep it simple, stupid"), is still the best advice. For all communications the sender should consider:

- What am I trying to say?
- Whom is the message for?
- How should it be sent so that it can be understood as quickly as possible?

# TUESDAY

The simple answer is to concentrate on clarity and brevity. Whatever the issue, the purpose of business communication is to get things done or to help create favourable environments for getting things done at a later date. But the enemies of purpose, clarity and brevity lurk throughout the business community. These enemies are management attitudes and the cult of evasive language.

*Management attitudes*

Management, and in particular British management, is very suspicious about communication. Most managers recognise in principle the need for communication with staff, suppliers and customers. However, in practice, they lack confidence and are concerned about the need to know, leaks to the competition or the press, and the possibility that premature announcements will leave them looking foolish. As a result, many corporate communication programmes become one-way vehicles for propaganda.

Management hates to convey negative information – for example, possible redundancies resulting from recent mergers – since it believes that it is bad for business and for staff motivation, but it consistently underrates the intelligence of its audience who usually know more about the business than is envisaged. On the other hand, good news propaganda is easy to identify. As a result, much of corporate communication only succeeds in breeding mistrust and cynicism.

Finally, managers are bad listeners. They have been taught that their role is to lead, but that concept has been interpreted to mean that seeking subordinates' views or listening to others is some diminution of the leadership role or even an attack on their status. Perhaps the most important skill that needs to be encouraged in the national school's curriculum and most certainly in business schools is the ability to *listen*.

# TUESDAY

*Evasive language*
Technical jargon and 'business-speak' cause confusion, but there is also the more dangerous variant of deliberately evasive language. An executive statement that 'We are reappraising our communications culture to bring our decision-makers closer to our customers' which really means that the workforce is to be 'downsized' by 40 per cent, is bad enough. A company report that refers to the death of thousands of people from chemical poisoning as 'the incident at Bhopal' is verging on obscenity. A wilfully distorted message is also an insult to the intelligence of the recipients of that message.

A recent study of company reports showed that abstract, evasive language is a sure sign that the company is doing badly. Successful companies are those that have the confidence to send out clear messages. Plain English pays.

## Summary

Today, we have looked at the methods and media we use to communicate. We examined the changes being brought about by new technology. These were changes in the growth of information we have to handle and changes in the way we work because of the need to communicate and manage information. We also noted the need to formulate our communication messages in the manner best suited to the intended recipient.

On Wednesday, we shall look at communicating with the most important of business recipients: our customers.

# WEDNESDAY

## Customer focus

Business survival, let alone success, depends on strategies, products and services that are directed at delighting customers. This statement is a truism which most executives readily accept. Unfortunately, not enough realise that to achieve that level of customer focus, they need to *talk* to customers. They believe that they know the business and therefore know what the customer wants. But customer perceptions of their own needs are constantly changing.

The diagram overleaf indicates the degree to which customer perceptions have changed since the onslaught of global competition. In the 1960s the sellers' market meant that customers were satisfied if the product just worked most of the time. The Japanese changed that customer perception, and the expected requirements began to include the way customers were invoiced, the way queries were handled and other elements of service surrounding the product.

# WEDNESDAY

Increasing competition and the resulting rise in customer expectations has now reached the current level of delight or excitement felt by the customer. The way the customer is communicated with is an essential feature of that excitement.

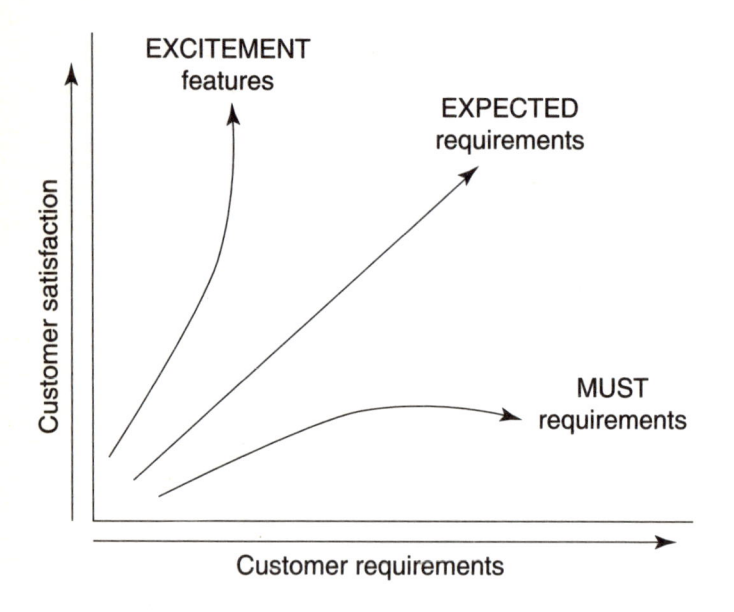

Figure 9: *Customer quality perceptions*

An experience with Virgin Atlantic Airways provides a good example of what is meant by customer focus. A customer of Virgin's Upper Class service was waiting for the limousine that Virgin provide to and from the airport when he received a telephone call from Virgin: 'Mr Macdonald, we are sorry to tell you that your flight to Boston will be delayed by up to two hours. Would you prefer to spend that time at home or be picked up immediately?' The none-too-pleased customer opted for the time at home, and the Virgin representative continued: 'We have noted from your ticketing that you were

# WEDNESDAY

using Boston as a transit stop on the way to Chicago. We have checked with our Boston people, and we are certain that we can make that connection. We will handle your baggage separately, you will be first off the plane and our representative will meet you and take you through VIP immigration to your connecting flight.' The customer has now moved his perception from annoyance at inconvenience to being impressed with Virgin's attempts to put things right. Then followed the customer focus. Their representatives had stepped into the customer's shoes and envisaged the issues surrounding the delay. 'Sir, with your planned stopover, had you intended meeting or phoning colleagues in Boston? If so, could we (Virgin) phone them and explain that it was our fault that you couldn't.' A dissatisfied customer has now become a delighted customer. There were no bribes or sweeteners to keep the customer happy but instead a series of communications both within the organisation and to the customer to ensure the excitement feature. That is customer focus. It comes from that old-fashioned virtue of *knowing* the customer and attending to his or her *personal* needs. Customer focus comes from that customer knowledge.

## Key elements of customer communication

Communicating with customers has to be a considered, planned and organised activity. Too often, management is satisfied only with the quick-fix solution of customer-care training for receptionists and others who talk directly with customers so that they are courteous and caring. This will not suffice in today's competitive marketplace. Here, we will concentrate on the four key elements of customer communication, namely:

# WEDNESDAY

> 1 *Marketing* – who are our customers, and what are needs and desires?
> 2 *Promotion* – letting the customers know that we have solutions to their needs;
> 3 *Selling* – agreeing, and contracting, to meet the personal needs of individual customers;
> 4 *Service* – providing the after-sales service and care that creates lifetime customers.

Conventional wisdom tends to combine the first three elements as disparate parts of marketing. That is, however, a major fallacy in business.

*Marketing*
Marketing is responsible for researching and defining customer needs and wants, and then for designing the products and services that will delight customers. Marketing has little or nothing to do with promoting or selling products and services. Thus, research and development is part of the marketing function but selling is not.

The communication methods used by the marketing department to carry out its primary functions can be summarised as follows:

- Customer and market surveys
- Customer focus groups
- Relations with 'special' customers
- Competitive intelligence
- Benchmarking
- Database techniques

# WEDNESDAY

*Customer and market surveys*

Consumer surveys and questionnaires are the most prevalent method of seeking customer and prospect views because they:

- are cheap
- are relatively easy to organise
- are easy to process
- provide demographic data

However, this form of communication is only partly effective. Customer surveys rarely provide the level of input required. Unless the customer experience has been very bad, the overall input is generally good enough to create a feeling of comfort. However, a new competitor could dramatically change the survey evaluation. Surveys suffer fom generalisation, whereas marketing strategy is dependent on specifics.

A survey gathers quasi-factual information and demographic data for analysis. It also allows a limited feedback from the customer, and may help to identify future members of focus groups. However, the approach suffers from a lack of interaction with the recipients, and takes little account of their perceptions. Customer perceptions about the use of data linked to their identity can lead them to fantasise or even lie about own their status and desires.

Some of the above weaknesses in surveys can be overcome by the careful formulation and juxtaposition of questions, but usually at the cost of sacrificing brevity. At best, this method of communicating with customers should be used sparely, and only to indicate trends or to identify areas for more in-depth research. As we shall see later, technology now provides more powerful tools for collecting useful data.

# WEDNESDAY

*Customer focus groups*

The focus group is one of the most powerful communication tools available to marketing. It can provide both subjective and objective information. By their very nature, focus groups *involve* the customer both in research and, to some extent, in decisions. Competently managed, they can provide an intuitive perspective which can be as relevant as the analytical data. The successful management of customer focus groups is dependent on three areas:

1 *The composition of the group:* the first determinant for selection of the group members is the intended *focus* of the marketeer. This will range from an overall evaluation of perceived service to the acceptability of an intended new product. The set-up will therefore vary between a group representing the overall customer base to a more tightly selected group representing a specific market sector.

   Experience has shown that seven to nine members constitute the most effective focus groups. Focus groups are not to be confused with market opinion groups. The latter are designed for relatively large audiences that provide more interaction than do written questionnaires.

2 *The organisation of the venue:* we want to encourage discussion and elicit opinions rather than deliver information. This requires a relaxed and non-confrontational environment. The advice is to avoid formal boardroom-style layouts and 'threatening' devices such as tape recorders. On the positive side, provide constant informal access to light refreshments.

3 *The selection of the facilitator:* facilitating *meaningful* discussion is a highly skilled competence which requires training and experience. If that expertise does not exist in the organisation, seek outside help.

## WEDNESDAY

*Relations with special customers*

All businesses have key account customers who provide a combination of revenue and market credibility, and as a result are accorded special attention. There is nothing wrong with this, but it can be a source of conflict between selling and marketing. The sales force aims to keep the customer focussed on the immediate sales situation. It wants to keep close to the customer and control all communication. Outsiders, such as marketing, are seen as a complication to be avoided. Marketing sees the same customers as providing a 'partnership of interest' in defining the future , and thus also wants to 'get close'. Both functions have laudable objectives but they can appear to be in conflict. Here, the chief executive has a crucial role to play in resolving any perceived conflict and in ensuring successful communication with the special customers.

*Competitive intelligence*

# WEDNESDAY

Competitive intelligence is not to be confused with industrial espionage. Knowing the 'other side of the hill' has always been essential for the world's leading companies. Of the two elements of gaining and analysing intelligence, the first is clearly a communications exercise. A whole book could be devoted to this subject, but from the author's experience, a useful start would be to combine an ambitious new MBA graduate and a qualified librarian within the marketing department. The former has knowledge of business and an eager desire to 'find out', and the latter has the professional training required to manage information.

*Benchmarking*
Benchmarking is a communications device for identifying the best practices and adapting them to your own organisation. This process is described in a companion book in this series, *Understanding Benchmarking*.

*Database techniques*
The convergence of technologies is increasing the scope of customer communication, even though some of the devices involved are not perceived as being related to communication. In retail outlets, point-of-sale devices combined with bar-coding techniques, have helped to develop detailed data on the behaviour of millions of customers. Such database information allows the continuous matching of the broad pattern of customer decisions to the goods on the shelf. This use of communication is to the advantage of both parties.

Tesco have now taken this concept into new realms with the launch of its Clubcard. Although this is a loyalty or discount card rather than a credit card, it uses similar technology to *personalise* the information that Tesco collects

# WEDNESDAY

for its customer database. In only six weeks, Tesco built up more than five million detailed personal records of *individual* customer decisions. Individual customer preferences or buying patterns can be tracked and identified across the whole range of products; store by store. As a result, customers can be invited to special events or offered special opportunities which are directly related to their preferences. Even 'lost' customers can be identified and strategies devised to entice them back. One of the world's largest supermarket chains is now able to act like a local shopkeeper who 'knows' the customer. This capability has had a major impact on their business performance but would have been deemed impossible only a few years ago.

*Promotion*
Promotion is primarily a communications function. Its role is to gain the attention of possible customers and let them know that the organisation can meet their desires. The various activities included under promotion can be summarised as:

| | |
|---|---|
| advertising | public relations |
| promotional events | publications |
| packaging and display | direct mail |

Depending on the nature of the business, each of these activities will be used for a different purpose. They may be designed to elicit a direct buying response from the prospect or to create an environment for the sales function. This is not the book to describe each of these activities in detail, but there are some principles of communication with customers which are relevant to them all.

# WEDNESDAY

We started today by considering customer perceptions, and the diagram on page 48 indicated the growing need for 'excitement features'. There is a dangerous temptation for promotional operations to meet this need by inventing the excitement. In fairness, they can also be led into this practice by the claims of marketing about a new product, as for example with the fiasco over Unilever's claims about the new power of Persil or Omo. There are regulatory bodies to control some of these claims, of which many are relatively toothless.

A principle of the marketplace (the arena for communicating with customers) is: All that customers want is what they have been promised.' Promises are made to customers in promoting and selling products and services, and management should be alert to *dubious* promises made in advertising, packaging and other promotional activities. Almost without exception, false promises made in the excitement of the moment come back to haunt the organisation. They also cost a lot of money: the quick buck now is usually paid for later.

## WEDNESDAY

In communicating with customers, promotional or marketing flair should not be confused with false promises. Imagination and flair are essential and positive elements in successful communication. The 'white paint war' of a few years ago provides a perfect example of such flair. For a long period the paint market was dominated by the perceived need to be the 'whitest.' Reflective agents were added to paint, and advertising copywriters came up with 'whiter than white.' These were impossible parameters to communicate to customers, and so inevitably the whole market became involved in a costly price war. Then, with a touch of pigment and an intuitive feel for customer perceptions, an ICI marketing manager created 'not quite white' which could be sold at a higher price. She transformed ICI's profit margins and market share, and all ICI's competitors then played follow the leader.

On Sunday, we saw that successful business communication must be carefully planned and organised. On Tuesday, we noted that the media often becomes more important than the message. Both these points demand that the purpose of the message should be clear to the sender before it is formulated. This is an important principle in promotional activities (and in particular in advertising) where the formulation of the message is often in the hands of outside consultants. Clients are prone to be entranced by the clever slogan or formulation of the message rather than by its real purpose.

The American airline company Delta recently provided a subtle example of the divergence between the purpose and the formulation of a message. Delta's advertising copywriters devised the slogan 'Delta – we love to fly ... and it shows'. Everyone at the company loved the new slogan, and it

# WEDNESDAY

appeared on every form of promotion used to communicate to customers. But one customer received bad service from Delta and remonstrated with its management that the slogan demonstrated that Delta had forgotten the purpose of its business: not to fly planes but *to move people by air.* A senior executive listened to the angry customer, and despite their advertising agency, the slogan was changed to 'You'll love the way we fly' – a subtle but powerful change of emphasis from the sender to the recipient.

*Selling*

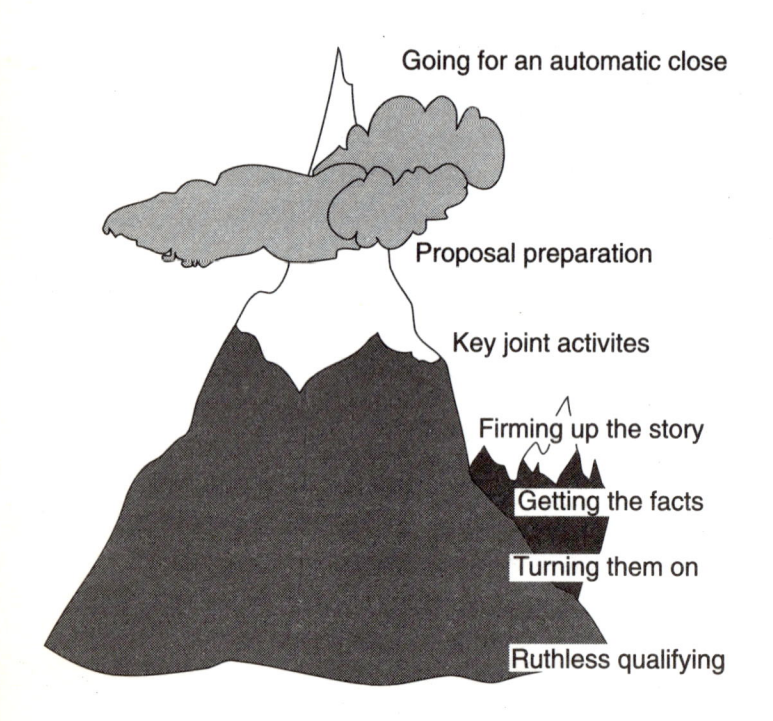

Going for an automatic close

Proposal preparation

Key joint activites

Firming up the story

Getting the facts

Turning them on

Ruthless qualifying

Figure 10: *Successful selling*

# WEDNESDAY

Successful selling is usually based on careful planning and organisation. It has been likened to climbing a mountain by a series of communication steps culminating in a favourable decision on the part of the customer (see Figure 10). Having said that, a sales person also has to communicate persuasively, and to this end, he or she should concentrate on the indirect channels of communication and create a favourable environment by developing certain personality characteristics.

- The visual personality – appearance, stance, poise, gestures and facial expressions
- The audible personality – voice, diction, intentional pauses, variation in pace and tone
- Cultivating the human qualities of warmth, sincerity friendliness, humour, courtesy, tact and helpfulness
- Achieving and maintaining audience contact through interest, enthusiasm and attention

*The five Cs of successful communication*
This is an appropriate moment to introduce the five Cs of communication:

1 Clarity
   - Avoid using ambiguous words
   - Use simple sentences for complex ideas
   - Give frequent illustrations (analogies, examples)
   - Make reference to people as well as to things
   - Use the language of the listener or reader
   - Restate your ideas (repeat yourself, using different words)
   - Make only one point at a time
   - Let the listener know your subject or solution at the start

# WEDNESDAY

2  Conciseness
   - Brevity minimises the chance that you will be boring or misunderstood
   - Trim the fat
   - Watch out for those rambling, strung-out sentences
   - They can confuse when speaking and are even more deadly when writing
   - Use short rather than big words
   - Translate wordy phrases into brief equivalents
   - Keep to at least 70 per cent one-syllable words
   - Use the active rather than the passive tense

3  Character
   - Compete for the recipient's attention
   - Express your personality – communication comes from people, not machines
   - Talk about *persons* as well as systems and things
   - Use down-to-earth colloquialisms and figures of speech (i.e. add colour to black and white talk)
   - Use humour where apposite

4  Courtesy
   - Courtesy is an attitude of mind underlying action
   - Courtesy is not a polite social convention or a veneer applied to make your message attractive
   - Courtesy puts others before self – which means putting yourself in the other person's shoes and recognising their objectives

5  Control
   - Check whether the message has been received and the desired action has been taken – feedback
   - Feedback may require specific questions

# WEDNESDAY

The above apply equally to written or spoken communication.

*Service*
In today's highly competitive economy, service has become the key factor in customer loyalty. The Forum Corporation of the USA surveyed more than 2,000 customers from 14 different organisations. More than 40 per cent listed poor service as the main reason for switching to the competition. Only 8 per cent listed price.

Service is provided by people communicating with customers. Everything that we have discussed over the last few days applies to service. A more detailed guide to this element of business communication is contained in a companion volume in this series entitled *Successful Customer Care*.

## Summary

Today, we have considered communication with customers. We noted the changing perceptions of customers and the importance of customer focus. We then concentrated on the communication methods and issues relating to marketing, promotion, selling and customer-care service. Common to each of these functions were the five Cs of communication.

In all this discussion, we have considered only the external customer of an organisation. On Thursday, we turn to the internal customer.

# THURSDAY

## Employee focus

If we are to sustain the level of customer focus we discussed yesterday, there needs to be a similar focus on employee communication. The management should see employees as its internal customers who also have needs and expectations. It should also recognise that employees have a valuable knowledge of what is really happening in the organisation – they are the people 'making the boxes'. Successful communication between management and employees can forge a partnership of interest in delighting the external customers. Yet too often management and employees act as adversaries, with the customers the victims of this war. Even enlightened management can fall into the trap of communicating *at* rather than *with* employees. It recognises the need to keep employees 'in the picture', and it takes great trouble in formulating the message, varying the briefing media and encouraging feedback, but it still fails. Such employee communication systems are essentially one-way as it is management who usually sets the agenda.

For successful communication at work, management must provide the means and the *permission* for the employees to set some agendas of their own. Business needs open communication systems that allow speedy communication from the workers about the problems that they are currently facing or are anticipating – problems that will interfere with the objective of delighting customers. Organisations that ignore this facet will soon find themselves on the rocks.

## Communications strategy

Developing and implementing an effective strategy for two-way employee communication, organisation-wide, is dependent on the following elements:

- Creating and maintaining an environment or culture that will support employee communication
- Ensuring line-management comprehension, commitment and skills to support the strategy
- Empowering and involving the employee in implementing the strategy.

As we look at each of these elements, we should be aware that the specific actions involved will differ for each organisation: the prevailing environments will be unique, and the actions should always match the particular culture.

# T H U R S D A Y

*The culture*

The environment or culture of the organisation must be conducive to open and purposeful communication, or it will not thrive. The culture of an organisation is assessed from the day-to-day actions and behaviour of its members. These are governed by the *real* value systems, which are not necessarily those written down or expressed by its leaders. The environment is thus based on the *perceptions* which drive the actions of those involved, and these can be in direct conflict with the stated values. Some common examples illustrate the point:

| Stated value | Reality |
| --- | --- |
| 'We encourage open and frank communication' | 'We shoot the messenger – I don't want to hear about your problems, give me the solutions.' |
| 'We welcome employee involvement' | 'Great idea – but get on with your work.' |

## THURSDAY

| 'We value our customers' | 'Ship it – we need the revenue.' |
|---|---|
| 'Our employees are our greatest asset' | 'I want a 40 per cent reduction in our labour force.' |
| 'We encourage feedback – we want to know the views of our employees' | 'What do they know anyway? They are a bunch of cynics. That's what's wrong with British labour.' |

Organisational culture is established by how management acts rather than by what it says.

A communications strategy should therefore start with some form of assessment of both the real organisational culture and the barriers to successful communication. An approach to this type of assessment is explained in detail in a companion book in this series, *Understanding Total Quality Management*. The assessment should help to decide whether to develop a communications strategy to change the culture, or whether to use the prevailing culture to support and improve communication with employees.

The points to be covered in preparing a communications strategy can be summarised as follows:

- Developing or reinforcing a culture where values come to mean more than just words on a mission statement
- Communicating company values to support the strategy and to ensure that the organisation is open to change
- Ensuring that the strategy can cope with a vast amount of information and interfaces in times of change

# THURSDAY

- Achieving consistency in communication despite different cultural and language perceptions
- Using the strategy as an agent of change, and helping employees to understand both what will change and what this change will mean for them

*The implementation plan and line managers*
On Monday, we saw that executives are weak at communicating their decisions and vision to line managers. To overcome this barrier to communication, it is essential that the communications strategy be translated into a workable implementation plan. This plan should be sufficiently detailed to encompass the following requirements:

- Defining the media to be used for communication to employees *throughout* the organisation
- Ensuring that the technology *supports* rather than drives the communications strategy
- Ensuring that staff who do not have access to technology are at least involved with more conventional means of communication
- Ensuring that face-to-face communication is still a key part of the plan
- Providing the resources to support the plan

*The implememtation plan and employees*
The implementation plan should also take into account the following aspects of employee communication:

- Establishing a communications network
- Ensuring that the right message is delivered to the right people at the right time
- Eliminating conflicting messages
- Establishing meaningful measures

# THURSDAY

*The communications network*

Every organisation will already contain a communications network established by the employees to fill the vacuum created by the lack of open management communication. It is the gossip network here which can be powerful and highly effective. Unfortunately, this is fed by rumour and false messages, and as such can also be dangerous and destructive to employee morale and attitudes. The best way to counter the gossip network is to implement a communications network which empowers employees to give feedback and ensures that this feedback is demonstrably acted upon. In particular, the network should:

- Allow information, questions, comments and opinions to travel through the organisation
- Ensure that managers have the answers to questions, and that they indicate where and how information will be available

# THURSDAY

- Build employee trust in the communications process so that honest feedback becomes a part of the natural way of working
- Remember that humour can break down many perceived barriers
- Overcome the barriers to communication associated with the differing perceptions of the recipients in different divisions, locations or parts of a unit
- Create an understanding both of different roles and of the need for collaboration in the organisation by encouraging discussion and debate between employees in different functions and at different levels

*The right message*
We noted on Sunday the importance of using channels of communication to create an identity of interest between the sender and the recipient of a message. Nowhere is this more important than with employee communication. This means that the sender (for example, management) must:

- Decide who should receive the message, according to the information to be communicated
- Know the perceptions of the employees or recipients to ensure that the message is relevant
- Continually question to check that the *right* message has been communicated and received
- Correct immediately any misinterpretation of the message

*Eliminating conflicting messages*
Management is prone to send messages to external audiences, such as shareholders and customers, that are different from those sent to employees, and the meanings of these different messages are often in conflict.

## THURSDAY

The implementation plan should therefore define actions to align internal and external communication systems and agencies so as to eliminate this problem. The plan needs to:

- ensure that there is no conflict between the message that is given to employees and the one given to the external market
- ensure that the internal communications operation and the public-relations department collaborate and give equal weight to internal and external communication
- realise that bad internal messages and gossip will eventually reach external recipients also
- ensure that the employees' trust in the internal channels of communication is not broken by their hearing messages *first* via external channels
- ensure that the internal and external communication policies both stem from the same strategic considerations

*Establishing meaningful measures*

What you cannot measure, you cannot manage. This is as true for so-called 'soft projects' as for other business performance areas. The criteria for the meaningful measure both of the effectiveness of the communications strategy and of the benefits it brings to the business should be established from the outset and be included in the plan. They should cover the following activities:

- Tracking the extent to which messages have reached all the intended recipients
- Measuring (by interview or questionnaire) the degree of understanding of the message, the changing perceptions and attitudes of employees, and the behaviour and communications skills of managers

# THURSDAY

- Ensuring that the measures are realistic and focus on a few specific areas at a time
- Relating the measurement trends and results to the overall business performance

## Sustaining the communications strategy

Many initiatives in business are launched with enthusiasm but a year later seem to have 'died on the vine'. They have become yet another flavour of the month as the management focus changes. To avoid this scenario, the chief executive or another senior executive should take ownership of the communications strategy and champion its implementation. The role of the champion here is to see that the initiative remains in focus despite the inevitable distractions. To this end, he or she will:

- continually update and enhance the implementation plan as the employee's expectations increase
- avoid monotony by varying the media
- maintain managers' and employees' attention on techniques and actions introduced earlier in the deployment of the strategy
- ensure that other business pressures and priorities do not take precedence over the strategy
- maintain senior management's commitment to the communications strategy and ensure that management is not delivering conflicting messages
- monitor the indirect channels, to ensure that management action matches the talk

# THURSDAY

## Management behaviour

A successful employee communications strategy will ultimately depend upon the behaviour of the line managers. Managers who listen to the views and interpretations of those involved are better placed to make the right implementation decisions. They are also likely to have a better understanding of employee attitudes, and are thus better placed to remove the barriers to communication that we discussed on Monday.

An employee, whose opinion has been honestly sought and listened to is much more likely to respond positively to management messages. If the reasons for decisions are clearly explained, individuals will most often respond enthusiastically, even if the decision runs counter to their opinion. They also have self-esteem because they have been recognised and treated with respect by their managers.

There are three important elements in ensuring that management behaviour supports the employee communications strategy:

1  Gaining management commitment
2  Training managers in communication skills
3  Making management communication a measure of managers' performance.

Let us examine each of these in turn.

*Gaining management commitment*
Management commitment will not come from instructions or a motivational speech. It will only come from management comprehension of the *need*, to change its behaviour, and this comprehension is likely to convert into

# THURSDAY

ownership of the need, and appropriate action. The management's transition to leadership requires comprehension of its changing role of coach, mentor and communicator. The executive champion should take the lead in:

- Indicating to line managers that information does not equal power, and encouraging them to share information with their staff
- Demonstrating to managers that the messages coming up the organisation are as important as those going down
- Convincing management that suppressing bad news is more damaging than telling it
- Showing line management that openness and honesty will result in increased trust from employees and enhance their credibility
- Ensuring that line managers do not retain or file information due to pressure of work
- Encouraging managers to adapt (not change) messages to relate to local perceptions
- Illustrating to line managers that better-informed, motivated employees will help them to meet their objectives

*Training managers in communication skills*
Most line managers believe that training their people in communication skills is a worthwhile exercise. Unfortunately, they also believe that they are in their posts because they are good communicators, and that they themselves, therefore, don't need training in these skills. There is a tendency for managers to believe that their role is to make decisions and then communicate these to the employees. In their own mind, the word 'communicate' is a synonym for 'tell'. Successful communication at work is designed to ensure both better

## THURSDAY

decisions and collaboration in implementing these decisions. It is not designed to remove the responsibility for policy or decision-making from management; indeed, it is the role of management to help people to achieve work tasks. However, the very best managers will also recognise that they need help from their people.

The most essential element in management development is to instill the belief in managers that they are now leading; a belief that will provide an inner confidence or self-esteem so that they are prepared to be vulnerable. It is also important to understand that disagreement, openly expressed, from peers or subordinates is not necessarily a sign of disrespect. Confident managers realise that 'soft' or caring management does not mean weak management. A manager who seeks others' views, even strong disagreement, before making and explaining a decision, will win respect and intense loyalty from employees. That is leadership, not mere management.

The education and training of managers must therefore include the elements of comprehension and commitment that we noted on page 71. However, managers also need the competence that comes from training in the specific skills needed to be a good communicator:

| | |
|---|---|
| analysing messages | understanding the communications model |
| presentation skills | listening skills |
| leading teams and meetings | delivering a brief |
| body language | recognising and understanding how people interpret messages |

*Performance measurement*
Management will keep focussed on the importance of communication if its performance measurements include a measurement of its level of competency in communication skills. Initial and appraisal interviews should ensure agreement on the communication competencies included in the specific job profile. Competency in employee communications should be an essential element in recognising management performance. The concept of 'upward appraisal' can be helpful in maintaining this focus.

## Empowerment of employees

Empowerment means giving employees the responsibility, authority and resources to act on their own initiative in a growing arena of business operations. By definition, this should also change the way senior management traditionally communicates with employees. Empowerment also implies that the employees have been given *permission* to communicate with management about the problems they are encountering in meeting their new responsibilities. We are now therefore considering two-way communication about an employee-determined agenda.

Earlier, we noted the barrier of language in achieving real two-way communication. The key to solving this problem is to establish the common language of measurement to aid objective communication about issues and problems. Traditionally, management has seen measurement as a tool to control work and workers. In the changed circumstances of the information age, the most effective step that management can take in the empowerment of employees is to allow them to measure rather than to be measured.

# THURSDAY

The continuous measurement – and the *display of the measures* – of the work processes in which the employees engaged can change the whole culture of an organisation. All the previously hidden frustrations and hassle related to work are now open for discussion in an objective environment.

There is nothing esoteric in this simple solution to many of the problems in business. All it needs is a commitment to the thorough education and training of both management and employees in the concept and practice of appropriate measurement in their business operations. Measurement is not only an important element in two-way communication, it is also the outward sign of inward grace for the successful organisation.

# THURSDAY

## Teamwork

Teamwork is the basis for a whole new way of working towards delighting customers and gaining a competitive advantage. Teamwork can be simply defined as management and employees working together to continuously improve their business processes. Successful communication is the glue that unites teams in a single purpose.

## Recognition

A confident and proud workforce will add colossal value to the overall performance of an organisation. An employee who enjoys confidence and self-esteem as part of a team feels pride in both his or her work and his or her company. Management recognition of the worth of employees as individuals is a determining factor in developing this attitude amongst employees.

Research has proved that recognition in its many forms is more important than rewards, including money incentives. A sense of worth gives meaning to the life and work of the individual. There are many different types of recognition, and these must be selected to suit the individual and the circumstances. They encompass praise, more responsibility and authority, professional recognition and a sense of accomplishment in the work situation. Recognition is reinforced when it is then communicated to peers and others involved with the individual.

# THURSDAY

When recognising individuals for their contribution in the workplace, it is also important to recognise their worth to others in their outside environment. Recognition that involves the family, friends and others in the individual's community is doubly effective in establishing self-esteem and confidence.

## Summary

We have spent Thursday considering the various elements involved in two-way communication with employees. We looked at:

- How the customer focus depends on the employee focus
- Developing a communications strategy
- Culture and environment
- The implementation plan
- The communications network
- Avoiding conflict and designing the right message
- Meaningful measures
- Sustaining the communications strategy
- Management behaviour, commitment and training
- Empowerment and teamwork
- Recognition

Tomorrow, we turn our attention to communicating with others outside the organisation.

## FRIDAY

# External communication

Organisations do not exist or work in a vacuum. There are many outside organisations, groups, interests and individuals who can influence/limit our business performance. On Wednesday, we discussed external communication with actual and potential customers. Today, we will consider our relations and communication with outside parties including:

- Suppliers
- Providers: owners, shareholders or the electorate
- Regulatory bodies
- Special interest groups
- The community at large

## Suppliers

Traditionally, communication with suppliers has been adversarial in nature. Purchasing departments or agents aim to buy at the lowest possible price, and all trust between the parties is gone, sacrificed on the altar of short-term profit. Now, however, more and more companies are recognising that this approach to suppliers is counterproductive, though having said this, areas of the public sector which are being driven by so-called 'market factors' have still had a tendency to follow the outdated traditional approach of lowest tender only.

## FRIDAY

Managers should try to reverse roles and consider their own position as a customer of their suppliers. Can their organisation help its suppliers to correctly anticipate the latter's own needs? It is just possible that the suppliers have the same problems in determining the needs of their own customers as do the managers.

Major corporations such as Marks & Spencer, Compaq and J Sainsbury establish long-term relationships with their suppliers on the basis that they share common interests and goals. These companies recognised years ago that pressurising suppliers on price by using the weight of their buying power was against their best interests since awarding purchase contracts on price alone inevitably meant compromising quality. These corporations also realised that a host of problems involving suppliers are caused by the ordering company, usually through evasive or fuzzy communication.

# FRIDAY

Partnerships of interest cannot be established with a horde of competitive suppliers for each product. How would the buying company react towards its own customers if orders were fragmented or switched arbitrarily to maintain price pressure? This approach ignores the cost of evaluating new suppliers and the time lost in changing from one supplier to another. Multi-supply also introduces greater variation into work processes and thus works against the objective of *reducing* variation. Companies committed to continuous improvement are demanding the same from their suppliers. The first step on that path is to move towards single sourcing and then help the chosen supplier to meet the buyer's objectives. This entails open communication based on the concept that the supplier wants to do a good job – indeed the supplier wants to delight the customer.

Close collaboration with suppliers should be a planned two-way communication exercise. Selection will obviously take into account technical and financial competence, but it should also be extended to consider the personality and culture of the supplying company:

- Will it be able to share similar principles and values?
- How does it value its workforce?
- How well does it communicate, both internally and externally?
- Is it prepared to change with us?
- Is it likely to make a good long-term partner?

The answer to the last question will partly be answered by the degree to which both parties have been able to reach an identity and established trust during communication. Successful communication with suppliers can make a major contribution to improved business performance.

## Providers

Every organisation is dependent on an investment of financial resources into implementing its strategy and plans. In the commercial sector, these resources are provided by owners and shareholders. In the public sector, the resources ultimately come from the electorate. It would be unwise for an organisation to omit these providers from its communications strategy.

Each type of provider will have its own characteristics which need to be taken into account in planning communication, but they all have one thing in common: they all want to know what the organisation is doing with their money. The presentation of financial accounts, business performance and forecasts are thus a major factor in communicating with providers. However, like all types of communication, these presentations must take into account the perception of the recipients.

# FRIDAY

*Owners*
Owners may be individuals, a family or another company. They will tend to have much closer contact with and day-to-day interest in the company than general shareholders. In many cases, indeed, these providers will initiate the communication, usually in a questioning mode. As each situation will be unique, there are no special points to make other than to say that all the rules of the communication model apply.

*Shareholders*
For the purposes of planning communication, shareholders can be divided into institutional shareholders and private shareholders. It is also important to pay attention to the parties that influence investors, such as brokers, analysts and the financial press.

Most public companies are effectively owned by a small number of institutions, and according to Richard Hews of Ludgate Communications, there are a number of far-reaching trends that are currently at work which can affect institutional attitudes:

- Institutions are consolidating to form even larger organisations able to take bigger blocks of shares in companies and, as a result, to exercise greater influence over those companies
- Some large institutions are prepared to invest significantly in under-performing companies in order to stimulate, and if necessary enforce, change when this is seen to be desirable

# FRIDAY

The company's communications with its institutional shareholders must therefore be very closely focused, involving direct and frequent contact with the fund managers and analysts who advise it. By the same token, the institution should have access to top management. Remember that the single most important criterion influencing an institution's decision to invest is its perception of the quality and potential of a company's senior management.

Every shareholder is influenced by the financial press, and the latter should therefore be a key target of the communications strategy. Get to know the relevant journalists and their editors, and tailor your communication to their needs. Contrary to some perceptions, financial and business journalists will give a company a fair hearing if approached at the right time with respect, professionalism and concise, timely and accurate information. Financial PR specialists can be of great help in effective communication with the press.

Brokers and their analysts form another critical part of a communication plan for shareholders since they write influential research notes on companies for both institutional clients and for the financial press. Similarly, analysts can quickly provide an informal view of a company's performance for major shareholders. It is therefore sensible for the company to get to know and develop communication with a number of analysts.

While there is no substitute for good performance, careful attention to the needs and requests of analysts and the press will create an understanding and appreciation of corporate strategy. This can soften criticism and generally enhance a company's image.

# FRIDAY

Private shareholders receive the reports and accounts of the company and are invited to the annual general meeting, and more regular contact can be designed to promote interest in the operations of their company. They will be influenced by the financial press, advertising, targeted discounts and special offers for the company's products or services. Shareholders can be invited to in-house company events and provided with a regular newsletter.

Informing the electorate can be a complicated issue. Many organisations have issued a simple statement only to be caught in the crossfire from party political conflict. If the intention of the communication is to support a particular policy of one political party, make this support clear without rancour or emotional argument. Remember that next time may involve a new policy and another party. In general, be aware of the political nuances in dealing with the electorate, and keep to simple facts and examples.

## Regulatory bodies

Every organisation is constrained/protected by various regulations that usually emanate from some form of public authority or professional body. Some of these regulations, such as the Health and Safety at Work Act, apply to everyone whilst others, such as beef bans or General Medical Council regulations, apply only to specific organisations. Some typical regulatory bodies include:

| the European Commission | local-authority bylaws |
| --- | --- |
| food and drugs administration | the ministry of agriculture |

## FRIDAY

| | |
|---|---|
| the ministry of health | the inland revenue |
| customs and excise | the law courts |
| professional and trade associations | other government ministries and agencies |
| similar overseas bodies | consumer associations |

Many of the current environmental regulations on pollution were resisted fiercely at their inception but are now accepted. This resistance is understandable as many of these regulations impose onerous costs of compliance on those being regulated. A small proportion of regulations, however, are downright stupid and reflect a total ignorance of the situation. These are usually the result of a mindless bureaucracy.

## FRIDAY

The vast majority of regulations are published in some form of draft before they become 'law'. Organisations should monitor these drafts so that they are in a position to communicate their viewpoint or take into account other opinions that could help in formulating the regulations in the most favourable context. Large corporations are likely to use permanent consultants and lobbyists to ensure that their positions are protected. Small companies should anticipate regulations in collaboration with their representatives in their trade association, chamber of commerce or for example wider bodies such as the Institute of Directors, and then encourage these bodies to lobby on their behalf. This is another area to be included in the communications strategy to ensure that at the very least the issue is not neglected and that the resulting regulations do not come as a great surprise.

## Special interest groups

There are a growing number of special interest groups competing for the attention of companies and the media. Many are 'worthy causes' requesting support, or more specifically donations, irrespective of whether or not their cause has anything to do with the business. Others, however, can create undesirable publicity or steadily build up perceptions until they reach 'crisis' proportions.

Charitable donations are a straightforward issue of policy, and can be viewed as the passive element of community relations. The policy issues are related to the amounts donated, the selection that brings the greatest benefit and the degree of empowerment granted to the local operation to

## FRIDAY

make its own decisions based on local knowledge and priorities. Only the board of the company can decide on the thorny issues of, for example, political contributions.

An individual organisation or company may become involved or targeted as part of a campaign by a special interest group without notice or reasonable expectation. This can involve the company spokespersons in a conflict with the media for which they are ill equipped. During a major crisis, it quickly becomes apparent that events can be driven by the media. The task of management is to take control of the situation by being prepared and by anticipating the needs of the media. The rules are similar to those noted for dealing wih financial journalists, and they can be summarised in this context as follows:

- Understand media deadlines and media needs
- To answer 'no comment' will only encourage the journalistic imagination
- From the outset, stick to the 'known facts'
- Make no assumptions or guesses: they will come back to haunt you
- It is acceptable to ask for time to check facts
- Always come back with promised feedback within the deadlines
- Simple professionalism which aids the journalist will pay dividends

As with all issues of communication at work, handling the media and crisis confrontation need prior thought and planning. You may not be able to anticipate the exact nature of a crisis, but you can at least plan crisis management in communications. Some of the factors involved are as follows:

# FRIDAY

- How to contact executives and key specialists during non-working hours?
- Where is the best location for a media centre, and how should it be equipped?
- How to gather the relevant facts?
- Selecting and training credible media spokespersons
- Finally, stick to the facts and the truth. The media are highly experienced in recognising contradictions and unearthing internal sources of information. Business people are not accomplished liars and usually get caught out in the end

## The community at large

Active involvement in the community, as opposed to the easy passive option of 'sending a cheque', is becoming an important issue in the marketplace. With greater selectivity in employment, companies are conscious that any reputation they gain in the community will help them attract the best potential staff. Major retailers have taken the lead in proactive community involvement. The 'Side by Side' initiative of J Sainsbury is typical of the best in the field. This involves the identifying of a number of organisations and getting groups of Sainsbury's staff to meet them and see what they can do and how they might help. Apart from the contribution to the community, Sainsbury believes that this initiative and its involvement programmes enhance the understanding, self-confidence and development of young managers.

For a large corporation, successful involvement and communication with the community depends on overall policy guidance and resources from the centre. This policy

# FRIDAY

will be deployed to provide a universal message to all employees, seeking ownership of the need and responsive local management that will develop actions that are tailored to local conditions. Although most organisations will be pleased to accept financial contributions, what they really value is recognition, friendship and real involvement.

## Summary

Today, we have looked outside the organisation and beyond our customers. We have recognised the long-term importance of anticipating events and of involvement with a series of outside bodies. We decided that a viable communications strategy should embrace:

- Suppliers – our business associates
- Owners in many forms – who provide the investment to realise our plans
- Regulatory bodies and special interest groups – who can impact our operations when least expected
- The community in which we live and operate

# S A T U R D A Y

# Keep talking and listening

Over the last week, we have seen that there are many ramifications to communication at work. We have stressed that business communication will not happen by accident, and that it is not a series of one-off events. Communication is a process rather than a programme.

The responsibility for developing a communications strategy and a corporate communications culture lies with the senior management or leaders of the organisation. As we have seen, to be successful, these will often require a fundamental change in management behaviour. Senior management must continually reinforce the focus on the communications strategy. None of this will happen just because the executives want it to happen. As we saw on Monday, the practice of management and corporate history have helped create many barriers to communication. Specific actions and resources will be required to dismantle these barriers and to create a communications culture. Some of these actions can be summarised as follows:

- Carrying out an assessment of the current communications culture
- Executive development of a communications strategy and value systems
- Executive and operational management development of an implementation plan
- Executives and other senior management learning to listen effectively

# SATURDAY

## Assessment

Every organisation has developed its own culture over time, and so starts from its own unique position. Before deciding on a plan, it is therefore important to measure where the organisation stands. An assessment will demonstrate the barriers to communication and provide a reasonable guide to the employees' attitudes to and perceptions of teamwork and participation. This form of assessment can be carried out relatively inexpensively by qualified consultants, and takes the form of tailored questionnaires supported by individual and focus-group interviews. Usually, it demonstrates the need for improved communication, and helps senior management to take ownership of the need to change.

## The communications strategy

The organisation may well have a mission or purpose statement and a published set of values which are deemed important. If so, the executives should meet to consider the degree to which these values are understood and practiced. If not, they should meet to establish the cultural leadership principles they espouse. In both cases, they should consider the part communications could play in ensuring business improvement. A broad strategy will define the key milestones along the lines discussed on Wednesday, Thursday and Friday.

# The implementation plan

One of the executives should agree to champion the communications strategy and maintain its impetus. The champion's first step is to select a representative group of operational managers and communication specialists to develop a detailed implementation plan. It is essential that this plan cover the education and training needed, key communication activities, responsibility for action and the measurable criteria for success. The completed plan must be agreed by the executives.

The education and training element of the plan should define the needs and curricula for all levels of the organisation. There are two elements involved here:

1 'Mindset change' education, which is a vehicle to develop 'buy in' to the values and the strategy
2 'Skill' training, to give to all the knowledge needed for successful communication

The knowledge required will include learning and practising the techniques which have been touched upon in this book. These include:

- Basic communication skills. *Successful Presentation* another book in this series, will also help here
- Communications-media knowledge. *Successful Public Relations* and *Successful Direct Mail* in this series are also valuable aids
- Skills in building teams, team leadership and teamworking.
- Effective listening skills

# SATURDAY

A large corporation may appoint a 'communications co-ordinator' to assist in implementing the plan. An objective of the strategy is to develop line managers who will take ownership of their own elements of the plan. Once this has been achieved, the role of the co-ordinator is over: if this post were maintained as a permanent separate role, there would be a danger of the line managers abdicating their role.

## Successful listening

As already mentioned, successful communication depends upon effective listening. A listening manager will soon:

- open the channels of communication and keep them open
- recognise subordinates' wider skills and ideas
- develop synergy and strong teamwork
- encourage innovation – 'thinking outside the box'
- increase employees' self-esteem and confidence
- improve the performance of the operation
- create commitment to both the job and the organisation

Every actual or potential manager should take part in an effective-listening and/or team-building course as part of the basic skill training for his or her job.

Another listening activity which is often abused is the 'management walkabout'. With too many managers, this degenerates into an exercise of the 'hail fellow – well met' variety. Management should see the 'walkabout' as a vital element in communications with employees. Used properly, it can be a very powerful form both of effective listening and of keeping in touch with the 'making of boxes'.

# SATURDAY

*Body language*

Listening, to be effective, must be supported by positive body language. Eastern cultures are better at listening than Western cultures, but Westerners feel uncomfortable when faced with the 'inscrutable Oriental'. The British are noted for their skill in using silence in their conversations, but when combined with their delight in 'poker-faced' humour it causes confusion to continental Europeans and Americans alike. They are not sure when the British are being serious or not. Effective and supportive body language will dispel this confusion.

Non-verbal communication by people is a complex process involving gestures, body posture, facial expressions, tone of voice and the way we are dressed. In terms of business communication, words convey information while body language conveys attitude. Non-verbal communication is also a complicated affair because people are wholly unaware of their body language and find it extremely difficult to change or control.

A helpful exercise in developing an awareness of the part body language can play in supporting or destroying the intended message is that of observation. Turn the sound down during a TV discussion and attempt to read the performers' postures. Again, watch an old silent movie in which the actors had only body language available as a communication skill. This will be over-emphasised, but it does show the power of indirect non-verbal channels.

Women are generally very good at reading body language. They appear to be more perceptive in picking up and deciphering non-verbal signals. Perhaps this is that innate ability known as feminine intuition.

# SATURDAY

## Setting the physical environment

We have discussed the cultural environment, but it is also worth noting the importance of setting the right physical environment for communication events. The first consideration is the suitability of the venue for the type and size of audience, and the ability to handle the appropriate media equipment to create the right atmosphere.

The role of music should not be ignored as a communications tool. It has a great power to influence mood and receptivity. Stirring marches can support a 'call to action' message, while there is a wide choice of music to provide a 'feel good' mood. This is not manipulation but using indirect channels to reinforce the message. No amount of manipulation can sell a bad message for very long. Interestingly, even the German Nuremburg rallies and similar propaganda events were only effective when the crowd was in a receptive mood, and it would be difficult for any British prime minister today to call for 'blood, tears, toil and sweat' the way Churchill did in 1940.

## Communications standards

Every organisation should prepare a guidebook to company standards for communication. This will ensure that all speak the same language through logos, visiting cards, brochures and events. Each employee should enhance the communications strategy and the company's intended image. A set of checklists for each kind of company event are of great help to those being called upon to organise them.

## Communications audits

A communications audit is an objective report on both the communications systems and the progress of the implementation plan. The audit will assist the senior management of the organisation in maintaining a clear focus on the communications strategy. Its timing and formulation should be included in the original plan.

## Summary

Today, we have considered:

- Senior management responsibility
- Communications assessment
- The preparation of a strategy and plan
- Successful listening
- Body language and environment

## Conclusion

This week, we have seen that communication at work is a major strategic element in business operations. Success in communication will require thought, dedication and continuous improvement. But it is worth it!